THE RIGHT KIND OF INTIMACY

(For God has me)

Sylvia M Dallas

http://sylviadallas.com

Photography by: Sylvia Dallas

Book cover (front) illustrated by ABLE
(http://iamableart.tumblr.com)

Published by: The Publisher's Notebook
email:publisher@thepublishersnotebook.com

International Standard Book Numbers:

- Ebook: 978-976-95691-5-7
- Hardcover: 978-976-95961-3-3
- Paperback: 978-976-95691-4-0

DEDICATION

This book is dedicated to the Holy Spirit, who is my Comforter, my Teacher and witness to my spirit of all things that are of God.

John 14:26 - But the Comforter, which is the Holy Ghost, whom the Father will send in my name, He shall teach you all things; and bring all things to remembrance, whatsoever I have said unto you (KJV)

Table of Contents

PREFACE

Sylvia Dallas, formerly known as Gina Rey Forest, had an encounter with her Saviour and was transformed to ensure that her talent of poetry writing gives glory to the Lord, the El Elyon God.

Her compilation of these poetic works speaks of the intimacy she developed with her God. She speaks to us clearly in her writings and we become so enticed as to move to the place of intimacy, becoming so intertwined with Jesus.

A true dedication to the Lover of our souls.

Courtney G Morrison
Pastor, Fellowship Tabernacle Portmore

Acknowledgements

I acknowledge the following people in my life who have been my support throughout this transition that I have experienced:

My husband Rohan.

My daughter Christina who has proven herself to be a blessing especially during my really rough times. My grandchildren Ashane, Chrisann, Joel and Warren.

My sisters Carol and Marjorie and my mother - Alice Walker.

Pastors Courtney and Caren Morrison.

Pastor Howard Tyson and his wife Janice.

Melvin Pennant and his wife Renee.

My church family especially Sodene, Yolanda, Auntie Carol, Letty, Vivienne.

My friends Michelle (Yapple Dapple), Marian, Zen and many others who encouraged me in this pursuit of happiness.

Truly the joy of the Lord is my strength.

Introduction

I made my name in poetry as Gina Rey Forest, sensuous poet. All my poetry including some very biting social commentary had a sexual and sensual reference. It became such a hallmark that it would not matter what kind of poetry I performed, I would still be introduced as the "sensuous poet". I have always hated being put in a box.

I began to get bored. I felt stained, even defiled. I sought the Lord about why I felt this way. I reasoned that I never promoted casual sex, I always promoted the concept of a relationship. However I chose to rationalise it, I could not feel satisfied.

I realised that all of my poems portrayed a desire for intimacy, but the source from which I sought it was wrong. This was a revelation for me, and so I decided to start over. I came to recognize that the only source of true love is from God Himself. I decided to seek intimacy with God from whom I had strayed. At last - satisfaction, fulfillment and finally peace.

I hope that these poems bless you as they have all been inspired by the closeness I have developed with my Heavenly Father.

THE RIGHT KIND OF INTIMACY

(For God Has Me)

Sylvia M Dallas

In the Closet

There was just no space
Not even a little bit
Even I tried to fit there
In my closet
Only to find junk.

And You visited me
From time to time
Told me You were seeking
A dwelling place With me
But there was no space

No space
Not even for me
Much more for You
Each time You said
"If you just move that out of there
I could find somewhere
To sit and talk with you"

"O no! Not that" said I
"I cannot part with it
Sentiments attached
I'm sure You understand"

And You did

Understand

That I valued things
More than Your company
That soul ties and past sentiments
Meant more to me
Than Your presence.
And You just stood outside the door
Gently knocking
Waiting for even the slightest
encouragement
An invitation to come in

And soon I realised
These "things" brought me
No pleasure
No companionship
Cold and empty they were
Devaluing my real estate of worship
No garage sale!! No!

Just a great bonfire
To which these "things" were consigned
A great big roaring flame
As even the cords that bound
Became loosed, broken and destroyed

I opened the door
And in You came

The darkness was lit
And the closet swept clean
Soon there was space for You

And me

To sit and talk

The Right Kind of Intimacy

My pen was an instrument
With which I sought to describe
intimacy
With the use of innuendo
And double entendre
But employed a means of deception

Not quite saying it out loud
Just taking the imagination
Of the crowd
Along for the ride with cryptic codes
Used in my odes to lust
Feigning innocence
As they dug beneath the surface
To grasp the real meaning

Hoping to convey the search
For intimacy,
For relationship
But using the wrong setting
And the oohs and ahs
Encouraged me
To believe the lie.
Yet some deep part of me
Remained unsatisfied

Unfulfilled and yes,
Defiled.

Then the realization
That lust has no true
Place with love.
It encourages only
The physical contact
Imitating the spiritual purity of love
But just for a moment.

Then I asked
"Why do I feel so soiled
After each recital?"
"After the climactic experience
Of the adulation of the crowd,
Why this need to wash myself
Until I can feel clean?"

So I learned to desire
Yes, desire to seek
The source of love
The source of this purity
That will not leave me feeling
As if I fell in a miry pit
That I had to claw my way out of

My desire led me to want
Arms that comforted

And made me feel safe
A refuge of strength and might
A freeness to worship
And courage to fight

My desire is to You
Always my Lord
For Your Holy Spirit
To be one with mine
So wedded to me
That one look at me
And all would see
YOU.

My desire is for Your peace
To hear Your sweet whispers
And Your encouraging words
For Your guidance and
The ordering of my steps

My desire is the intimacy
I have sought but
From the wrong source
And having found You
I will not let go.

Love Encounter

My heart quickens
It feels as if it would burst
So overcome with passion
Wrought from an encounter with You

I lean into your embrace
As I rest my head
Upon Your bosom
The sound of Your heartbeats
Echoes
Reverberates
Like thunder

I feel
Vibrations
Pulsing
Throughout my body
And even into my spirit
As our heartbeats
Find a unified rhythm

Coming into agreement
Of a great union with You
My soul knows very well
Its real

It's trustworthy
This outpouring of love
From Your heart to mine

My spirit has caught on
To a divine rhythm
I am ruined for any other sound
Any other beat
I can never be the same again.

You Care

If You did not care
Would you know
The number of hairs
On my head?

If You can dress
The flowers of the field
With such splendor
What would You
Not do for me
Whom you have made
Just a little lower than angels?

If birds of the air
Need not worry
About provision
Then why should I
When Your heart's desire
For me
Is the best
That You have

That You care about
Every detail of my life
Is evident in the fact

That You would ensure
That I Your beloved child
Gets sweet sleep
That You provide guardians
So that my feet shall not
Be dashed against a stone
You know my every need
Before I am even aware
And supply them in advance
Your favor provides a shield
Against onslaught of rejection
It makes me step out
In boldness knowing that
You are ever present
That You encompass me
On every side.

Your Bride

It is said that when two people
Embrace long enough
Their hearts beat in unison
So Holy Spirit
Embrace me continually

Let my heart declare
Your love for me
Lay my head
Upon Your bosom
And let the rhythm
Of Your heart
Set the pace for mine

As I reach up
To kiss Your face
With my worship
Let us dance in close embrace
To the music of heaven
A step by step
Arm in arm movement
Declaring the intimacy we share
Saying to the world
That I am Your bride

Come & See

I heard Him speak
And followed Him
And when He asked me
What was it that I sought
I said "Lord, show me where You live "
He said
"Come and see "

And I obeyed.

My joy in His presence
Could not be contained
I went seeking a friend
With whom to share
When I saw him I said
"I have found the Christ!
Come and see "

I saw another friend
Who told me about Him
He said his heart listened
When Jesus said "Follow me "
And together we went
And told other friends
"We have found a

Good thing out of Nazareth!
Come and see "

They who went to see Him
Realized that He already knew them
And each went to a friend
And proclaimed
"We have found Him
Who knew us
Him who redeemed us
Him who promised us
Open heavens because we believed

We found Him
Who stormed the gates of hell
And took back the keys!
Who heals the sick
Him who frees the oppressed
We have found Him
Who stills the storm
Walks on water
We have found Him!
We have found Him!
Come and see!"

Hallelujah!!!

In my pain
I cry a river of tears
But my heart whispers
Hallelujah

And my injured soul

Black and blue
From its torment
Lays prostrate
Before the seat of mercy
While my heart whispers
Hallelujah.

Mingled in my cries
Of pain
Are my whispers
Of praise
Hallelujah.

For I hang on tightly
To Your promises
The midnight of my terrors
Will only last for the night
For with the dawning
Comes joy.
Hallelujah!

Your Word is light
To my darkness
And the waters
Of my praise is troubled
As healing begins
Hallelujah!

My heart's whispers

Slowly make their way
Up from its deep recesses
Forming ripples on the surface
Bursting forth in bubbles
Coming forth in a rush
Coming forth as a shout
A declaration of joy in You
In it I find my strength
Hallelujah!! Hallelujah!!

Enter and Know Me

My Lord
Please come into my chamber of
worship
I have discarded the robes of my
righteousness
And perfumed myself with the oil of
gladness
I have dressed myself in garments of
praise

Enter

And as You are at the door
I wash Your feet
With my tears of joy
And embrace You

I want You to know me
To impregnate my spirit
With Your desires
I will joyfully nurture
Your Holy seed
And gladly labour
To bear Your fruit

O You give such
Sweet pillow talk

My ear is ever inclined
To Your lips
Your voice is like
The sound of many waters
That cause trembling
In my very spirit
My desire is for You
And You only

Know me
And cause me to know You also
Your touch is healing
Making broken threads like new

The trembling in my heart
My innermost being
Quickens as You embrace me
And keep me close

I am ever reminded
Of Your Presence
In everything I do
Everything I face
And I am safe with You

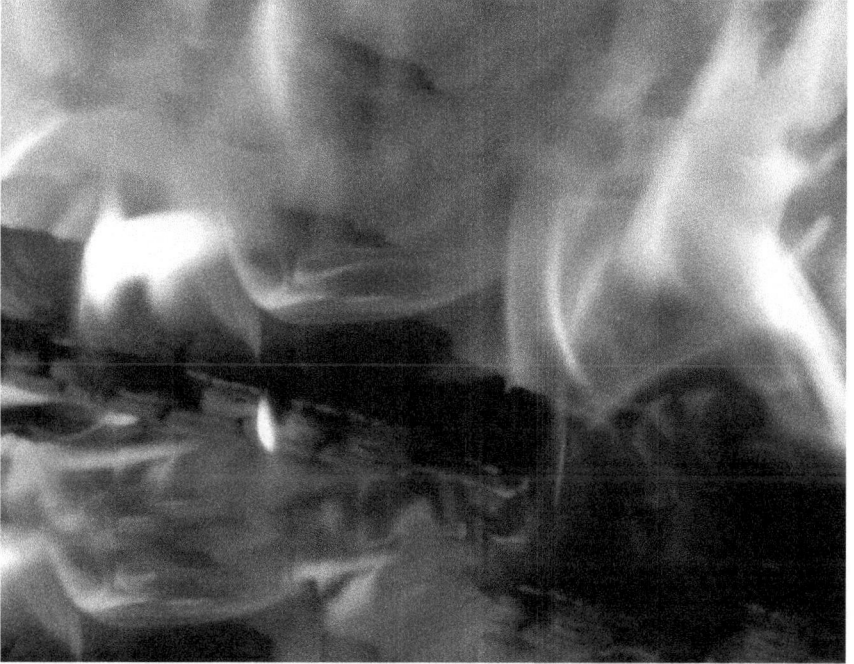

I AM

Be careful of what you see
When you look at me
See not the flesh
That has been threshed
On the floor of adversity
In pain and misery
See not that which is decayed
Buried and slayed

See instead the veil of red
That caused me to rise up from the
dead
And shake off the shroud from the
grave
As I emerged from the cave
To embrace life everlasting
And satisfying

See instead my stride of assurance
My battle stance
As I do the dance of victory
Trampling on the neck of you my
enemy
Even though you would have me
believe

That the battle has not been won
already

See Him
Yes! Jesus!
See Him
That walks before me
See Him
That causes me to declare
From my mouth without fear
Things that shall come to pass
As you look in wonder
At the favour that shields me

Because **I AM** made
In His image and likeness

I AM
Able to declare truth out of my mouth
Because of Him
To you my adversary I declare
I am not limited
By the shackles that you
Would use to try to bind my mind

Just like David
I will storm that city
Just because you say I cannot
I will lay siege
And starve you
From your position
Because there you won't find
Anything to feed on
As the fallow ground is broken
And purged of your seeds

I will use the hammer of the Word
To beat down your gates
I will uproot your foundations
With my battle cry
Joined with the shouts of the angels
In heaven

Just because
Through Him
I AM the conqueror
I AM the battle bow of God

When I declare a thing
It is established

I AM
The warhorse of God

Charging you
As I pierce your heart
With the arrows of His Word
Taking the violence to you
As you have brought it to me

Because of Him
I AM stronger than your forces
I shall see
One thousand falling on one side
Ten thousand falling on my right
And STILL you cannot touch me

Because of HIM!
I AM
Greater than sickness
An overcomer
Because of Him!
I AM able
To speak to mountains
And make them into plains
Remove the gates of your prison
From their foundations
And free nations

Because of Him!
I AM royalty
A king against whom

There is no uprising

Because of Him!
I AM
Able to invade your darkness
With His light in me
I AM
Able to break bows of steel
Though you surround me on every side
I AM
Delivered greatly

Because of Him!
I AM able to take that weapon
From you and slay you

Because of Him!
I AM
A mighty warrior of valor
I can break through your boundaries
And draw water from His well
There is no limit
To what **I AM**

Not in my flesh
Remember that has been threshed
Decayed and slayed
Buried in that grave

I AM risen
A new creation
Dressed in robes of righteousness
Donned in garments of praise

The old me is forever gone
What you see is
Not the weak and afraid
I AM delivered, sanctified and saved
I AM redeemed and esteemed
I have put on Christ
The strength I display
Is not mine
But His!

When you
My enemy comes to wage war
It is not with me
It is with Him!

Selah!

CHALLENGE!

Really?
That was your best shot?
You thought I would
Fall down and stay flat
Well my faith don't work like that
You have to come better than that

In the boxing ring
You thought it was me
You were fighting
But my King says
I don't have to do a thing
Except to cheer Him on
With my praising

So when you think
That you have me on the ropes
Giving me a pounding
Thinking that you have me
Where you want me
When you see me crying

It's not despair
It's joy from knowing

My deliverance is drawing near

Do not think
That as I curl up from the pain
That I am giving up hope
Because all I am doing
Is giving Him room to work
Because the weaker I am
The stronger He is
And as you see my mouth
Begin to open wide

You won't hear a cry of pain
Instead it will be a shout of PRAISE!

SONS OF GOD ARISE!

Arise O Sons of God
The Cup of Zanah
Is full to overflowing
The earth
Drenched with the blood of Innocents
And of Saints
Groans and swells
It is ready to burst forth
To cry out

Sons of God, ye watchmen
Why do you slumber
At the time of the watch?
Why hasn't the trumpet sounded?
The enemy has entered our gates
They have crept in unnoticed
And you lulled and deluded
Blasé and uncommitted
Have drunk from their cup
And ate at their table
You have not cried out
Against them
They have stained us
Soiled us

Sons of God

Are your eyes covered with scales?
Are your lips sewn shut?
Are you rooted in fear?
Is your armour rusted
From lack of care?

Gird your loins
And step out and declare
Serve notice on the Children of Pride
That the days of their king
Are numbered

Make a joyful noise
For the King of Glory cometh
He shall reward the humble
He shall forgive the repentant
He shall smite the wicked
And bend the necks of the proud
Prepare ye for His coming
Sons of God ARISE!!!

I CRY OUT TO YOU

In my anguish
Have I poured out my heart
In tears
My broken heart cries
For vengeance
Asking why?
WHY?

My flesh
Screams for me
To take matters into my own hands
To hurt and maim
But my spirit says
"Leave it to God"

My flesh says
"Pray for vengeance"
But my spirit says
"Trust God"
It says "He is just
He is righteous"

It says "look for Him
Keep Him in sight"

It says

"Remember
Who HE IS"
I choose to listen
To
My
Spirit.

GETHSEMANE

It is the dark night of my soul
Uncertainty wages war
With what I know to be true
Despair tries to find something in me
To cling to

I am afflicted to my very bones
In this wilderness
Voices foreign to me

Try to convince me

That You have forgotten me

And yet
Even though I am not hearing You
You have shown me
In little ways that You are there

I am trusting You
To lead me through this wilderness
I cannot find my way without You

The pain of not hearing You
Is far worse than the afflictions
Upon my body
And this agony
Is more than I can bear

Yet I say

Not my will but Yours
My heart will not stray
From You
I am broken
And trusting You
To make me whole

As the heat in this wilderness

Beats down upon me
I see the shade You have provided

And I rest in Your shadow
For I know Joy comes
With the dawning

He that believeth on me, as the scripture hath said, **out of his belly shall flow rivers of living water** - JOHN 7:38 (KJV)

"Behold, God is my salvation, I will trust and not be afraid; For the LORD GOD is my strength and song, And He has become my salvation." **Therefore you will joyously draw water from the springs of salvation.** 4And in that day you will say, "Give thanks to the LORD, call on His name. Make known His deeds among the peoples; Make them remember that His name is exalted ...... ISAIAH 12:2-4 (NIV)

Then the eyes of the blind will be opened And the ears of the deaf will be unstopped. Then the lame will leap like a deer, And the tongue of the mute will shout for joy. **For waters will break forth in the wilderness And streams in the Arabah.** The scorched land will become a pool, And the thirsty ground springs of water; ISAIAH 35:5-7 (NIV)

Ho! **Every one who thirsts, come to the waters**; And you who have no money come, buy and eat. Come, buy wine and milk without money and without cost. "Why do you spend money for what is not bread, And your wages for what does not satisfy? Listen carefully to Me, and eat what is good, And delight yourself in abundance.... ISAIAH 55:1-2 (NIV)

For it will be a unique day which is known to the LORD, neither day nor night, but it will come about that at evening time there will be light. **And in that day living waters will flow out of Jerusalem**, half of them toward the eastern sea and the other half toward the western sea; it will be

in summer as well as in winter. And the LORD will
be king over all the earth; in that day the LORD will
be the only one, and His name the only one....
ZECHARIAH 14:7-9 (NIV)

Praise Never Sleeps

Out of my belly
Comes a praise that never sleeps
A river of living water
That never rests
Not like a creek
But like a flood
A river in spate
That sweeps in
Removing debris
Smoothing the jagged edges
Of my heart

Out of my belly
Comes a praise
In tongues of the spirit
Communing with the Holy Spirit
Like the river
It flows swiftly
Uprooting the deeply rooted
Digging new channels
Making new pathways

Out of my belly
Comes a waterfall of praise
High above the earth
It brings down
The blessings of God

Fills the empty spaces
To overflowing
Creating tributaries
That flow continually

Out of my belly
Comes the praise
That sends forth

An invitation to my King
For His Word says
That He inhabits the praise
Of His saints
And when He comes
His glory shall fill
The hallways of His temple
And shine forth
Through the windows
Of my eyes

Out of my belly
Comes the praise
That is the war cry
Running down the skirmish line
Of warrior angel horsemen
Cheering on the troops
For His word declares
That the battle is not mine
But His

Out of my belly
Comes the praise
That declares the Word
That is the two edged sword
That executes the written judgment
That reaches the ends of the earth
A song of joy that causes God
To subdue the nations under my feet

Out of my belly
Comes the praise
That rouses God
To punish the nations
That sends the sharp arrows
Of God into the heart of His enemies
That causes God to ride out
victoriously
For the cause of truth and
righteousness

Out of my belly
Comes the praise
That is truth
It joins the heavens
In declaring His glory
It is the praise
That joins the earth

In trembling
It joins the sea in its roaring

That sings for joy
With the trees of the forest
It exalts His name on high

Out of my belly
Comes the praise
That is healing
That is deliverance
That is unashamed
That is blessing
That blesses His name
That blesses His works
That blesses my soul
That is continuous
And never ending

Testimony

I have often had reason over the last few years to review my life. Looking back at my poetry in 2007 I made a conscious decision and promise to God that I would not write another piece of poetry or go back on stage to perform unless it glorified Him.

A bold statement indeed, especially considering that immediately after I made that promise, I began to receive offers for paid performances and even inclusion in several magazines. I refused them all.

When I got married to the man I lived with for over five years, I heard a barely audible click, like a piece of puzzle had just been put in place. God be praised, my husband got saved on the very day we went for pre-marital counseling and so by the time we got married we were equally yoked. At the time of writing this preface I have been saved for thirty eight years. Yes - that's right 38 years. In that time I have done everything possible to rationalize the Word of God to suit every disobedience.

I have struggled most of my life with rebellion, stubborness, anger - you name it. However, on that day of July 22, 2011, I heard that audible click. For every stage of spiritual development after that I have heard that click over and over again, as God proceeded to mold me through deliverances, trials, teachings, putting the missing pieces of the puzzle that is my life in their proper places. It was as if He was just waiting patiently like the father in the story of the prodigal son, for my return so that He could bestow gifts and blessings upon me.

With a humble heart, I thank Him for His patience and love.

SYLVIA M. DALLAS
August 25, 2013

Contact Information:
Telephone: (876) 833-6722
Email: Publisher@thepublishersnotebook.com
Blog: http://sylviadallas.com
Twitter: @syldallas

Excerpt from AND THE PRISONERS HEARD THEM - Your Life of Praise Can Bring Freedom To Others

Written by Sylvia M Dallas

AND THE PRISONERS HEARD THEM

"And at midnight, Paul and Silas prayed and sang praises unto God: and the prisoners heard them" – Acts 16:25 KJV

Picture this. You are an unsaved person, and you keep hearing about this God that brings joy, peace and love. You have friends who say that they are Christians but you have yet to see any evidence of joy in their lives. All you can hear about is how difficult life is, they hardly ever smile and never have anything positive to say. Why on earth would you want to embrace the Christian life if this is the evidence of it?

As Christians we are supposed to be evangelizing, going out into the world and making disciples of all men according to the instructions we received in the Great Commission.[1] This means we are to preach the good news of the Gospel and drawing people to Christ. How can we achieve what is required of us if our spirits are downcast, if our countenance is low? Would you be attracted to the lifestyle of the person above? I think not!

Paul and Silas after being accused were locked in the deepest part of the dungeon and this was after they had just had "many stripes laid upon them " and "their feet fast in stocks"[2]. So beaten, placed in the inner part of the prison with their feet made immovable, they did the most unlikely thing...they began to pray and out of their prayers came praises which they sang unto God, doing the very thing for which they were jailed.

So you are in the dungeon, experiencing the similar conditions and a strange sound reaches your

---

[1] Matthew 28: 19-20 KJV
[2] Acts 16:22-24 KJV

ears. "Who in their right mind could be singing in this place, at this time of the night?" "Are they aware that this is a prison?" "Isn't that sound coming from the innermost part of the prison where the worst punishment takes place?" Here you are in your most miserable of conditions and someone in a worst position is singing? At first, you would probably wonder if the conditions they are experiencing have gotten to their heads. As you listen, you realize this is not the crazy maniacal sound of someone slowly going off their rocker. This is pure unadulterated joy.

You cannot understand it, but as the sound penetrates your mind, it touches something deep inside of you and you listen. You want to catch the rhythm. Suddenly you find yourself swaying to the beat. You don't know the song but deep down something bubbles up inside of you. You feel as if there is a foaming fountain coming up from within your belly. As you continue to listen, a shout escapes you, you become somehow involved in what is happening and you feel tremors. Something earth shaking, soul shaking is taking place. You don't know what it is. You have never experienced anything like this before, but you definitely feel it and you know change is coming. Suddenly your chains are loosed, broken off of you, fallen to the ground.

Your praises to God are not just for you. Your praises need to be heard by others to bring deliverance to them. The praises to God from you cannot remain in your thoughts, they must come from the utterance of your lips to bring change to someone's life – not just yours. At the midnight of your life, beaten and chained to immovability, when you think that you are at rock bottom, you have no idea where the next meal is coming from, how you are going to make it the next day, facing life or death surgery, facing deathlike situations – trust God and praise Him.

Your praises can bring about the greatest move of evangelism in your life. Trials are always an opportunity to demonstrate God's power. When someone who is not saved sees you praising your way through your situations, sees you feeding yourself with the Word, sees the manifestation of God's peace in your life, they see you sleeping, unmoved by the storm and they wonder "how can I get some of that peace?" They move from "how can I" to "I want", and before you know it you are being asked "where do you go to church?"

Years ago, I went to visit a friend at her home. As the day passed and I was enjoying my time with her, there was a knock on the door. When she answered, there were about five policemen with a search warrant. I was told that I could not leave, nor was I allowed to make any calls. Well I just simply turned around, lay down on the carpet and went to sleep. This was not a restless, tossing and turning kind of sleep. This was deep comfortable, snoring kind of sleep. I woke up periodically and they were still there every time I woke up. The last time I woke up, one of the policemen asked me how come I am able to sleep. I told him that I was at peace because I know I was not involved in anything. He allowed me to leave.

When you praise, you are at rest. All the encumbrances become loosed from your life and the enemy can find nothing in you.

"And suddenly there was a great earthquake, so that the foundations of the prison were shaken; and immediately all the doors were opened, and everyone's bands were loosed." - Acts 16:26 KJV